C000115620

ABOVE EVERY NAME

Thirty Contemporary Hymns
in Praise of Christ

TIMOTHY DUDLEY-SMITH

music editor:

WILLIAM LLEWELLYN

CANTERBURY
PRESS
Norwich

Published in the UK in 2009 by the Canterbury Press Norwich,
St Mary's Works, St Mary's Plain, Norwich NR3 3BH
Website: www.scm-canterburypress.co.uk

ISBN 978-1-85311-978-1

Also by the same author and available from Canterbury Press:
Beneath a Travelling Star: thirty contemporary carols and hymns for Christmas
A Calendar of Praise: thirty contemporary hymns for seasons of the Christian year
High Days and Holy Days: thirty contemporary hymns for annual occasions
in the life of the local church
The Voice of Faith: thirty contemporary hymns for Saints' Days
or based on the liturgy

Cover design by Leigh Hurlock
Music Engraving by William Llewellyn, Devon, UK
Typesetting by Regent Typesetting, London
Printed in England by Barnwell Print Ltd., Aylsham, Norfolk NR11 6SU

Contents

Where, throughout the collection, suggested alternative tunes contain a cross-reference, the letters *CP* signify *Common Praise*, SCM-Canterbury Press, 2000.

1 Name of all majesty

MAJESTAS 66 55 66 64

Michael Baughen *b.*1930
arranged Noël Tredinnick *b.*1949

1. Name of all ma - jes - ty, fa - thom-less mys - te - ry,

King of the a - ges by an - gels a - dored;

power and au - tho - ri - ty, splen - dour and dig - ni - ty,

bow to his ma - ster - y, Je - sus is Lord!

NAME of all majesty,
　　fathomless mystery,
King of the ages
by angels adored;
　　power and authority,
　　splendour and dignity,
　　bow to his mastery,
Jesus is Lord!

2　Child of our destiny,
　　God from eternity,
　　love of the Father
　　on sinners outpoured;
　　　see now what God has done
　　　sending his only Son,
　　　Christ the beloved One,
　　Jesus is Lord!

3　Saviour of Calvary,
　　costliest victory,
　　darkness defeated
　　and Eden restored;
　　　born as a man to die,
　　　nailed to a cross on high,
　　　cold in the grave to lie,
　　Jesus is Lord!

4　Source of all sovereignty,
　　light, immortality,
　　life everlasting
　　and heaven assured;
　　　so with the ransomed, we
　　　praise him eternally,
　　　Christ in his majesty,
　　Jesus is Lord!

2 Jesus, the saving Name

i

CARLISLE SM

Melody and most of the harmony
by Charles Lockhart 1745-1815

1. Je - sus, the sav - ing_ Name! As - cend - ed,_ glo - ri - fied,_

he reigns who_once for_ sin - ners came, and once for_ sin - ners died.

ii

FALCON STREET SM

Melody by Isaac Smith 1734-1805

1. Je - sus, the sav - ing Name! As - cend - ed, glo - ri - fied,

he reigns who once for sin - ners came, and once_ for sin - ners died.

Jesus, the saving Name !
　　Ascended, glorified,
he reigns who once for sinners came,
　　and once for sinners died.

2　Eternal Lord most high,
　　and with the Father one !
His Name angelic voices cry,
　　the everlasting Son.

3　Salvation's source and strength !
　　In Jesus' Name we prove
the depth and breadth and height and length
　　of God's redeeming love.

4　Unwearied grace divine
　　to take the sinner's part !
May Jesus' Name in glory shine
　　on every contrite heart.

5　So lift on high his praise,
　　the Saviour's love proclaim,
and all the songs of all our days
　　be 'Glory to his Name !'

3 Wonder of all wonders

Trier Gesangbuch 1847
Harmony by Charles Wood 1866-1926

TRIER 68 888 44

1. Won-der of__ all won - ders! that Christ should lay a - side his crown

and to a fall - en world come down, and in a sta - ble

bleak and bare should choose our hu - man life__ to share,

and all__ for love, for God__ is Love.

WONDER of all wonders !
that Christ should lay aside his crown
and to a fallen world come down,
and in a stable bleak and bare
should choose our human life to share,
   and all for love,
    for God is Love.

   Wonder of all wonders !
that he to whom by right belongs
the praise of countless angels' songs
should be the child the shepherds saw,
the Lamb of God amidst the straw,
   and all for love,
    for God is Love.

   Wonder of all wonders !
that clear upon the cloudless skies
a star should shine to lead the wise,
whose myrrh and frankincense and gold
a kingly sacrifice foretold,
   and all for love,
    for God is Love.

   Wonder of all wonders !
this child within the cattle stall
is he who died to save us all;
the risen Lord whom Mary bore,
whose life is ours for evermore,
   and all for love,
    for God is Love.

4 Gold for a manger bed

GOLD FOR A MANGER BED 65 65 66 65

William Llewellyn *b*.1925

1. Gold for a mang-er bed, Je-sus en-shrin-ing; straw where he lays his head, soft-ly re-clin-ing; so small and still he lies as on his in-fant eyes high in the

dark - ened skies_____ the stars____ are shin - ing.

G OLD for a manger bed,
Jesus enshrining;
straw where he lays his head,
softly reclining;
so small and still he lies
as on his infant eyes
high in the darkened skies
the stars are shining.

2   King and Creator see,
whose hands have wrought us;
Saviour and Shepherd he,
who loved and sought us;
our God in human frame
who to a lost world came
and on the cross of shame
so dearly bought us.

3   Gold for a monarch's state,
all things sustaining;
High Prince and Potentate,
death's dread disdaining;
to him the ransomed raise
unceasing songs of praise,
through everlasting days
in glory reigning.

Alternative tune: MONK'S GATE (*CP* 621)

5 Light of the world, true light divine

VASEY 886 D

Anne Harrison *b.*1954

long-a-wait-ed__ Light.
lives for ev-er-more.
all-pre-vail-ing__

Love.

im-mor-tal Life, un - fad-ing Light, and all-pre-vail-ing__ Love.

rall.

L IGHT of the world,
  true light divine,
in glory break
  and splendour shine
    upon our nature's night!
The darkness dies
  before the morn
and God himself
  a child is born,
    the long-awaited Light.

2 Life of the world,
     a life laid down,
   who chose the cross
     before the crown
       and opened heaven's door:
   he broke the chains
     of death and hell,
   our Saviour Christ,
     Emmanuel,
       who lives for evermore.

3 Lord of all worlds,
     a manger bed
   was room enough
     to lay your head
       when, from your throne above,
   you came to set
     a lost world right,
   immortal Life,
     unfading Light,
       and all-prevailing Love.

Alternative tune: MANNA

6 Beyond what mind can measure

Johann Steurlein 1546-1613
harmonized Healey Willan 1880-1968

WIE LIEBLICH IST DER MAIEN 76 76 D

1. Be - yond what mind can mea - sure or hu-man heart dis- close, in
Christ there lies_ the_ trea - sure that on - ly wis-dom knows. His
word of life dis - cern - ing, we stand on ho - ly_ ground; where,
writ - ten for_ our_ learn - ing, e - ter - nal truth is found.

B EYOND what mind can measure
   or human heart disclose,
in Christ there lies the treasure
   that only wisdom knows.
His word of life discerning,
   we stand on holy ground;
where, written for our learning,
   eternal truth is found.

2   A world of warring nations
     denies what God has willed:
for Christless generations
     their dreams are unfulfilled.
In learning, Lord, and teaching,
     may we our powers assign
to meet the minds outreaching
     in quest of life divine.

3   To hearts whose hope is sinking,
     to spirits bleak and bare,
to thought itself, where thinking
     is meaningless despair,
reveal again your glory,
     O God of grace and power,
and help us tell your story
     in ways to match the hour.

4   May he who died to save us
     renew the love we claim,
to spend the gifts he gave us
     in service of his Name;
till truth at last prevailing,
     in Christ the nations find
the Light and Life unfailing
     of every heart and mind.

7 Christ is the Bread of life indeed

Melody and figured bass
by Johann David Meyer 1636-1696
Edited by John Wilson 1905-1992

ES IST KEIN TAG (MEYER) 88 84

1. Christ is the Bread of life in - deed who nour - ish - es the hun - gry soul, the one on whom our spi - rits feed, who makes us whole.

CHRIST is the Bread of life indeed
    who nourishes the hungry soul,
the one on whom our spirits feed,
        who makes us whole.

2   Christ is the Door which open stands,
            the one who watch and ward will keep;
    the Shepherd of the heavenly lands
            who knows his sheep.

3   Christ is the Light of all the earth,
            to end our night of sin and gloom;
    the Resurrection-Life, whose birth
            has burst the tomb.

4   Christ is the living Vine, and we
            abide in him, who hear his call.
    The Way, the Truth, the Life is he,
            and Lord of all.

based on the seven 'I am' passages in St John's Gospel

Alternative tune: ALMSGIVING (*CP* 540)

8 Our living Lord whose Name we bear

Later form of melody by
Henry Carey c.1687-1743

CAREY'S (SURREY) 88 88 88

1. Our liv - ing Lord— whose Name— we bear,

whose home was once in Ga - li - lee,

who called— those first— dis - ci - ples there

to rise and come and— 'Fol - low me':

we hear a - gain your— call to - day

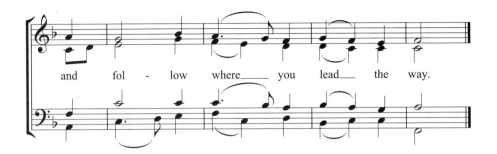

and fol - low where___ you lead___ the way.

OUR LIVING LORD whose Name we bear,
whose home was once in Galilee,
who called those first disciples there
to rise and come and 'Follow me':
we hear again your call today
and follow where you lead the way.

2 Our friend and guide whose fruitful word
is bread of life and living seed,
whose voice the people gladly heard,
as one who knew their deepest need:
we come to read and mark and learn,
and in your word your will discern.

3 Our Saviour Christ who for our sake
eternal glory laid aside,
and chose the path of pain to take,
and on the cross for sinners died,
may we, whose trust is in your Name,
to all the world your love proclaim.

4 Our Prince of life who died and rose,
and with the Father reigns above,
who by the Spirit lives in those
whose hearts lie open to your love,
your risen life be ours to share,
our glorious King, whose Name we bear.

Alternative tune: BOORT

9 Praise be to Christ in whom we see

From *Harmonia Perfecta* 1730
arranged by Alan Gray 1855-1935

BUCKLEBURY DLM

1. Praise be to Christ in whom we see the im-age of the Fa-ther shown, the first-born Son re-vealed and known, the truth and grace of de-i-ty; through whom cre-a-tion came to birth, whose fin-gers set the stars in place, the un-seen powers, and this small earth,

the   fur - thest   bounds   of   time   and   space.

PRAISE be to Christ in whom we see
    the image of the Father shown,
        the first-born Son revealed and known,
    the truth and grace of deity;
through whom creation came to birth,
    whose fingers set the stars in place,
the unseen powers, and this small earth,
    the furthest bounds of time and space.

2   Praise be to him whose sovereign sway
        and will upholds creation's plan;
        who is, before all worlds began
    and when our world has passed away:
    Lord of the church, its life and head,
        redemption's price and source and theme,
    alive, the first-born from the dead,
        to reign as all-in-all supreme.

3   Praise be to him who, Lord most high,
        the fullness of the Godhead shares;
        and yet our human nature bears,
    who came as man to bleed and die.
    And from his cross there flows our peace
        who chose for us the path he trod,
    that so might sins and sorrows cease
        and all be reconciled to God.

based on Colossians 1.15–20

Alternative tune: YE BANKS AND BRAES (*The Voice of Faith*, 10)

10 Prince of life and Lord of glory

Adapted by W H Monk 1823-1889
from a melody in *Geistreiches Gesangbuch*
(Darmstadt 1698) harmony slightly altered

ALL SAINTS 87 87 77

1. Prince of life and Lord of glo - ry, to whose Name be

love and praise; Son of God, whose hu - man sto - ry

touch - es all our earth - ly days, still our guide and

teach - er be, as of old in Ga - li - lee.

PRINCE of life and Lord of glory,
  to whose Name be love and praise;
Son of God, whose human story
  touches all our earthly days,
    still our guide and teacher be,
    as of old in Galilee.

2 Crowds who came where Christ was preaching,
    in the hills or by the shore,
  wondered at his gracious teaching,
    as no prophet taught before:
      where today your voice is heard
      tune our hearts to hear your word.

3 Mary's son, on earth revealing
    God himself in word and sign,
  toiling, travelling, teaching, healing,
    love incarnate, love divine,
      come as Shepherd of the soul,
      touch our lives and make them whole.

4 He who came for our befriending,
    selfless Saviour, Son of man,
  on the cross at Calvary ending
    all that Bethlehem began,
      Christ, who died to make us free,
      in your love remember me.

5 Risen Lord in glory seated,
    high-enthroned ascended Son,
  sinners ransomed, death defeated,
    all a world's salvation won,
      Prince of life, our lives sustain,
      till with you we rise and reign!

Alternative tune: GOUNOD

11 O changeless Christ, for ever new

ST BOTOLPH CM

Gordon Slater 1896-1979

1. O change - less Christ, for ev - er new,
who walked our earth - ly ways,
still draw our hearts as once you drew
the hearts of o - ther days.

O CHANGELESS Christ, for ever new,
who walked our earthly ways,
still draw our hearts as once you drew
the hearts of other days.

2   As once you spoke by plain and hill
or taught by shore and sea,
so be today our teacher still,
O Christ of Galilee.

3   As wind and storm their Master heard
and his command fulfilled,
may troubled hearts receive your word,
the tempest-tossed be stilled.

4   And as of old to all who prayed
your healing hand was shown,
so be your touch upon us laid,
unseen but not unknown.

5   In broken bread, in wine outpoured,
your new and living way
proclaim to us, O risen Lord,
O Christ of this our day.

6   O changeless Christ, till life is past
your blessing still be given;
then bring us home, to taste at last
the timeless joys of heaven.

Alternative tunes: WILTSHIRE (*CP* 604)
SALZBURG (Haydn, *CP* 536)

12 O Christ, who taught on earth of old

ST MATTHIAS   88 88 88

W H Monk 1823-1889

1. O Christ, who taught on earth of old, and fash-ioned in the tales you told of life and truth the hid - den key, and win-dows on e - ter - ni-ty, pre - pare our hearts, that in our turn we too may read and mark and learn.

O CHRIST, who taught on earth of old,
and fashioned in the tales you told
of life and truth the hidden key,
and windows on eternity,
    prepare our hearts, that in our turn
    we too may read and mark and learn.

2   The world of nature, death and birth,
the secrets of the fertile earth,
the ripened field, the garnered grain,
the seed that dies to live again,
    are doors in heaven, opened wide
    upon your kingdom's countryside.

3   Of wedding-feasts and pearls and flowers,
of debts, and half-completed towers,
of sunny slopes where vineyards grow,
we read more wisely than we know;
    for in your parables there shine
    the images of things divine.

4   A beggar's bowl, a robber band,
foundations built on rock or sand,
we mark them all; but one imparts
a dearer hope to human hearts:
    from that far country where we roam
    a Father's welcome calls us home.

Alternative tune: ABINGDON (*CP* 133)

13 O God of everlasting light

CLONMEL DCM

Irish Traditional Melody
arranged William Llewellyn *b.*1925

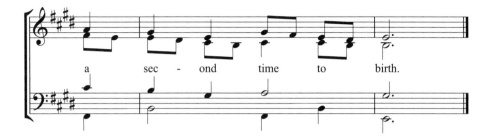

a sec - ond time to birth.

O GOD of everlasting light,
  whose boundless kingdom lies
beyond our world of sense and sight,
  unseen by mortal eyes;
we long to learn what Jesus taught
  that from this dust of earth
the seeking soul may still be brought
  a second time to birth.

2 Here may the springing waters flow
   to cleanse from every stain;
  here may the Wind of heaven blow
   to stir to life again.
  So freed from all the powers of death,
   from all our secret sins,
  and quickened by the Spirit's breath,
   our life in Christ begins.

3 O God of love, your Son you gave,
   we see him lifted high;
  your Son, who came to seek and save
   and on the cross to die.
  We name him Lord of life and love
   with all our ransomed powers,
  for born anew from God above
   eternal life is ours.

based on John 3.3–16

14 When Jesus lived among us

THAXTED 13 13 13 13 13 13

Gustav Holst 1874-1934
adapted from his Suite *The Planets*

1. When Je - sus lived a - mong us he came a child of earth

to wear our hu-man like - ness, to share our hu - man birth;

and af - ter flight and ex - ile, an a - lien re-fu - gee,

re - turn in peace and safe - ty at last to Ga - li - lee;

through sun - lit days of child-hood a lov-ing home to know;

in wis - dom and in fa - vour with God and man to grow.

W HEN Jesus lived among us he came a child of earth
to wear our human likeness, to share our human birth;
and after flight and exile, an alien refugee,
return in peace and safety at last to Galilee;
through sunlit days of childhood a loving home to know;
in wisdom and in favour with God and man to grow.

2   He came, the friend of sinners, to meet us in our need,
the gospel of his kingdom declare in word and deed,
to touch and cure the leper, the lost to seek and find,
to heal in signs and wonders the deaf and dumb and blind.
The voice of their Creator the wind and waters heard;
to those with ears to listen he spoke the living word.

3   'The Son of Man must suffer,' he taught by word and sign;
like bread his body broken, his blood poured out like wine.
His cross is for our pardon, our sacrifice for sins,
and by his resurrection our risen life begins.
We come in faith to Jesus to follow where he trod;
O Son of Man receive us, and make us sons of God.

15 Dear Lord, who bore our weight of woe

Arthur Somervell 1863-1937
from *The Passion of Christ* 1914

CHORUS ANGELORUM CM

1. Dear Lord, who bore our weight of woe
and for our par - don died,
in - cline our hearts to feel and know
those arms yet o - pen wide.

DEAR LORD, who bore our weight of woe
　　and for our pardon died,
incline our hearts to feel and know
　　those arms yet open wide.

2　Those loving arms enfold us still
　　　nor turn one soul away;
　　to him who welcomes all who will
　　　we come anew today.

3　In penitence and faith we come
　　　on Jesus' promise stayed:
　　of all our sin, the final sum
　　　for love alone he paid.

4　He paid what none may comprehend;
　　　what all have lost, restored;
　　the sinner's advocate and friend,
　　　our gracious loving Lord.

5　Our loving Lord! We rest within
　　　that Name all names above,
　　for vaster far than all our sin
　　　is Christ our Saviour's love

Alternative tune: BANGOR (*CP* 256)

16 No weight of gold or silver

MOVILLE 76 76 D

Irish Traditional Melody
harmonized by C H Kitson 1874-1944

Unison

1. No weight of gold or_ sil - ver can_ mea - sure hu - man worth;

no soul se - cures its_ ran - som with all the wealth of earth;

no sin - ners find their free - dom but_ by_____ the gift un-priced,

the_ Lamb of God un - blem - ished, the pre - cious blood of Christ.

NO WEIGHT of gold or silver
    can measure human worth;
no soul secures its ransom
    with all the wealth of earth;
no sinners find their freedom
    but by the gift unpriced,
the Lamb of God unblemished,
    the precious blood of Christ.

2   Our sins, our griefs and troubles,
    he bore and made his own;
we hid our faces from him,
    rejected and alone.
His wounds are for our healing,
    our peace is by his pain:
behold, the Man of sorrows,
    the Lamb for sinners slain!

3   In Christ the past is over,
    a new world now begins;
with him we rise to freedom
    who saves us from our sins.
We live by faith in Jesus
    to make his glory known:
behold the Man of sorrows,
    the Lamb upon his throne!

Alternative tunes: ARGENT
MORNING LIGHT (*CP* 578)

17 The love of Christ who died for me

IRISH CM

Melody from *Hymns and Sacred Poems*, Dublin 1749

1. The love of Christ_ who died_ for me
is more_ than mind_ can know,
his mer - cy mea - sure - less_ and free_
to meet_ the debt_ I owe.

THE LOVE of Christ who died for me
    is more than mind can know,
his mercy measureless and free
    to meet the debt I owe.

2   He came my sinful cause to plead,
        he laid his glories by,
    for me a homeless life to lead,
        a shameful death to die.

3   My sins I only see in part,
        my self-regarding ways;
    the secret places of my heart
        lie bare before his gaze.

4   For me the price of sin he paid;
        my sins beyond recall
    are all alike on Jesus laid,
        he died to bear them all.

5   O living Lord of life, for whom
        the heavens held their breath,
    to see, triumphant from the tomb,
        a love that conquers death,

6   Possess my heart that it may be
        your kingdom without end,
    O Christ who died for love of me
        and lives to be my friend.

Alternative tune: DUNDEE (*CP* 38)

18 Though one with God in form divine

LOVE IS YOUR NAME LM

William Llewellyn b.1925

1. Though one with God in form divine, by this the love of Christ is shown: he chose in mercy to resign his place beside the Father's throne.

THOUGH one with God in form divine,
    by this the love of Christ is shown:
he chose in mercy to resign
    his place beside the Father's throne.

2   He laid his kingly glories down,
    in self-surrender stooped to save,
and stripped himself of state and crown
    to bear the likeness of a slave.

3   Intent to do the Father's will,
    in human form and flesh he came;
and to the last obedient still
    he died in agony and shame.

4   Till from the dark of death's repose,
    the shuttered tomb, the midnight hour,
the Lord of life to glory rose,
    exalted by the Father's power.

5   To him, by God the Father given,
    that Name belongs, all names above,
a Name unmatched in earth or heaven
    for honour, majesty and love.

6   His Name let all creation bless,
    on bended knees in homage fall;
and to the Father's praise confess
    that Jesus Christ is Lord of all!

based on Philippians 2.6–11

Alternative tune: RIMINGTON

19 And sleeps my Lord in silence yet

from *Die Zauberflöte*
Wolfgang Amadeus Mozart 1756-1791

MOZART 88 88 88

1. And sleeps my Lord in silence yet, with - in the dark - ness laid a - way; where none re - mem - ber nor for - get, where breaks no more the sun - lit day? and sleeps my Lord in si - lence yet,

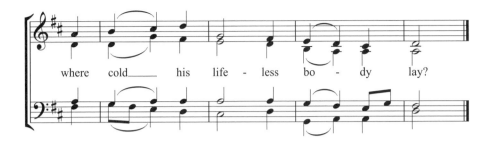

where cold____ his life - less bo - dy lay?

A ND SLEEPS my Lord in silence yet,
within the darkness laid away;
where none remember nor forget,
   where breaks no more the sunlit day?
and sleeps my Lord in silence yet,
   where cold his lifeless body lay?

2   And does the sting of death remain
     to work unchanged its bitter will?
were cross and passion all in vain,
     no battle won on Calvary's hill?
and does the sting of death remain,
     and gapes the grave in triumph still?

3   Have faith in Christ, the risen Son,
     who reigns eternal, glorified!
who death destroyed, who triumph won,
     who flung the gates of heaven wide!
Have faith in Christ, the risen Son,
     the living Lord of Eastertide!

suitable for Easter Eve

20 This day above all days

Keith Landis *b*.1922
harmonized William Llewellyn *b*.1925

MURRAY 66 86 66

1. This day a-bove all days glad hymns of tri-umph bring;

lift ev-ery heart to love and praise and ev-ery voice to sing:

for Je — sus is ris — en, our glo-rious Lord and King!

THIS day above all days
  glad hymns of triumph bring;
lift every heart to love and praise
and every voice to sing:
  for Jesus is risen,
our glorious Lord and King!

2 Christ keeps his Eastertide!
The Father's power descends;
the shuttered tomb he opens wide,
the rock-hewn grave he rends:
  for Jesus is risen,
and death's dominion ends!

3 What sovereign grace is found
in Christ for all our need!
The powers of sin and death are bound,
the ransomed captives freed:
  for Jesus is risen,
the Prince of life indeed!

4 So lift your joyful songs
with all the hosts on high,
where angel and archangel throngs
his ceaseless praises cry:
  for Jesus is risen,
and lives no more to die!

Alternative tunes: VINEYARD HAVEN (No. 26 in *A Calendar of Praise*)
LIMERICK

21 Now is Christ risen from the dead

ST FRANCIS (LASST UNS ERFREUEN)
LM and Alleluias

Melody from
Geistliche Kirchengesang (Cologne 1623)
Arranged by Ralph Vaughan Williams 1872-1958

Unison

1. Now is Christ ris - en from the dead, now

Harmony

are the powers of dark-ness fled, Al - le - lu - ia, al - le -

Unison

-lu - ia. Gone is the night of sin and gloom, Je -

Harmony

-sus is ris - en from the tomb. Al - le - lu - ia, al - le -

NOW IS CHRIST risen from the dead,
now are the powers of darkness fled,
Alleluia...
Gone is the night of sin and gloom,
Jesus is risen from the tomb.
Alleluia...

2   Now is Christ risen from the dead,
empty there lies his narrow bed,
Alleluia...
Christ and his cross have won the day,
come, see the grave in which he lay.
Alleluia...

3   Now is Christ risen from the dead,
he who his blood for sinners shed,
Alleluia...
In him who died to bear our sins
our resurrection-life begins.
Alleluia...

4   Now is Christ risen from the dead,
risen and reigning as he said,
Alleluia...
Praise him who light and life restored,
praise him, our ever-living Lord!
Alleluia...

22 Heaven's throne ascending

JESU, MEINE FREUDE 665 665 786

Melody from J Crüger's *Praxis Pietatis Melica* (1653)
as arranged by J S Bach (1685-1750)

1. Hea - ven's throne as - cend - ing, death's do - min - ion end - ing,

Christ the strong to save!   now in glo - ry seat - ed,

work on earth com - plet - ed,   ri - sen from the grave!

join   to praise through all   our days   Christ the   Lord of

love who sought us, and in dy - ing bought us.

HEAVEN'S throne ascending,
death's dominion ending,
 Christ the strong to save!
now in glory seated,
work on earth completed,
 risen from the grave!
join to praise through all our days
Christ the Lord of love who sought us,
 and in dying bought us.

2   Powers of darkness broken,
earth from sleep awoken,
 and to life re-born!
from our nature's prison
we with Christ are risen
 by that Easter morn.
Join to sing our glorious King,
risen, reigning, high ascending,
 Lord of life unending!

23 He walks among the golden lamps

i

REVELATION 86 88 86

Noël Tredinnick *b.*1949

1. He walks a-mong the gold-en lamps on feet like burn-ished bronze: his
hair as snows of win-ter white, his eyes with fire a-flame, and bright his
glo-rious robe of seam-less light sur-pass-ing Sol-o-mon's.

ii

WITHINGTON 86 88 86

John Barnard *b.*1948

1. He walks a-mong the gold-en lamps on feet like burn-ished bronze: his

hair as snows of win-ter white, his eyes with fire a-flame, and bright his

glo-rious robe of seam-less light sur-pass-ing Sol-o-mon's.

HE WALKS among the golden lamps
on feet like burnished bronze:
his hair as snows of winter white,
his eyes with fire aflame, and bright
his glorious robe of seamless light
    surpassing Solomon's.

2   And in his hand the seven stars
        and from his mouth a sword:
    his voice the thunder of the seas;
    all creatures bow to his decrees
    who holds the everlasting keys
        and reigns as sovereign Lord.

3   More radiant than the sun at noon,
        who was, and is to be:
    who was, from everlasting days;
    who lives, the Lord of all our ways;
    to him be majesty and praise
        for all eternity.

based on Revelation 1.12–18

24 Heavenly hosts in ceaseless worship

Eric H Thiman 1900-1975
from the anthem "Hark! a thrilling voice is sounding"

PARK CHAPEL 87 87 D

1. Heaven - ly hosts in cease - less wor - ship 'Ho - ly, ho - ly, ho - ly' cry;

'he who is, who was and will be, God Al - might - y, Lord most high.'

Praise and hon - our, power and glo - ry, be to him who reigns a - lone!

We, with all his hands have fash - ioned, fall be - fore the Fa - ther's throne.

HEAVENLY hosts in ceaseless worship
'Holy, holy, holy' cry;
'he who is, who was and will be,
    God Almighty, Lord most high.'
Praise and honour, power and glory,
    be to him who reigns alone!
We, with all his hands have fashioned,
    fall before the Father's throne.

2   All creation, all redemption,
        join to sing the Saviour's worth;
    Lamb of God, whose blood has bought us,
        kings and priests, to reign on earth.
    Wealth and wisdom, power and glory,
        honour, might, dominion, praise,
    now be his from all his creatures
        and to everlasting days!

based on Revelation 4 & 5

Alternative tune: ABBOT'S LEIGH (*CP* 418)

25 Kingly beyond all earthly kings

i

LLEDROD (LLANGOLLEN) LM

Welsh Hymn Melody

1. King - ly be - yond all earth-ly kings, Christ o - ver all, his

king - dom stands; our world, all worlds, the

sum of things, are held in be - ing by his hands.

ii

OMBERSLEY LM

W H Gladstone 1840-1891

1. King - ly be - yond all earth - ly kings, Christ o - ver all, his king - dom

stands;   our   world,   all   worlds,   the   sum   of

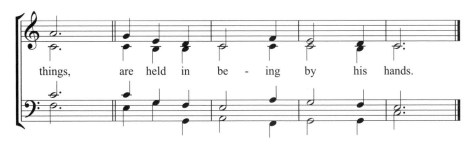

things,   are   held   in   be - ing   by   his   hands.

K INGLY beyond all earthly kings,
     Christ over all, his kingdom stands;
our world, all worlds, the sum of things,
     are held in being by his hands.

2   'King of the Jews', by Magi sought;
       'Blessed is he', the people cry;
   crowned as a jest and set at nought,
       'King of the Jews' he hangs to die.

3   Lord of all life and power he rose,
       King of creation's wide domain,
   soon shall the trump of God disclose
       Christ as the King who comes to reign.

4   Free from the bounds of time and space,
       yet of our inmost lives a part,
   both King and kingdom find a place
       enshrined in each believing heart.

5   'Your kingdom come' in this our day:
       hear us, O Lord; make haste and bring
   that reign of peace for which we pray,
       the righteous reign of Christ the King.

26 From the Father's throne on high

i

UNIVERSITY COLLEGE 77 77   Henry Gauntlett 1805-76

ii

ORIENTIS PARTIBUS 77 77

Medieval French Melody
harmonized by Ralph Vaughan Williams 1872-1958

FROM the Father's throne on high
    Christ returns to rule and reign:
child of earth, he came to die;
    judge of all he comes again.

2   Darkened be the day at noon
        when the stars of heaven fall:
    earth and sky and sun and moon,
        cloudy darkness covers all.

3   Ancient powers of sin and death
        shake to hear the trumpet blown;
    from the winds' remotest breath
        God will gather in his own.

4   So behold the promised sign,
        sky and sea by tumult riven,
    and the King of kings divine
        coming in the clouds of heaven.

5   Come then, Lord, in light and power,
        at whose word the worlds began;
    in the unexpected hour
        come in glory, Son of Man!

based on Mark 13.24–27

27 He comes to us as one unknown

Nicolaus Hermann 1485-1561
arranged and harmonized by J S Bach 1685-1750

NICOLAUS (LOBT GOTT) 86 886

1. He comes to us as one un - known,

a breath un - seen, un - heard;

as though with - in a heart of stone,

or shriv - elled seed in dark - ness sown,

a pulse of be - ing stirred.

HE COMES to us as one unknown,
  a breath unseen, unheard;
as though within a heart of stone,
or shrivelled seed in darkness sown,
    a pulse of being stirred.

2   He comes when souls in silence lie
      and thoughts of day depart;
    half-seen upon the inward eye,
    a falling star across the sky
      of night within the heart.

3   He comes to us in sound of seas,
      the ocean's fume and foam;
    yet small and still upon the breeze,
    a wind that stirs the tops of trees,
      a voice to call us home.

4   He comes in love as once he came
      by flesh and blood and birth;
    to bear within our mortal frame
    a life, a death, a saving Name,
      for every child of earth.

5   He comes in truth when faith is grown;
      believed, obeyed, adored:
    the Christ in all the Scriptures shown,
    as yet unseen, but not unknown,
      our Saviour and our Lord.

Alternative tunes: REPTON (*CP* 411)
BINNEY'S

28 As water to the thirsty

OASIS 76 76 66 44 6

T Brian Coleman b.1920

1. As wa - ter to the thir - sty, as beau - ty to the eyes, as strength that fol - lows weak - ness, as truth in - stead of lies, as song - time and spring - time and sum - mer - time to be, so is my Lord, my liv - ing Lord, so is my Lord to me.

AS WATER to the thirsty,
as beauty to the eyes,
as strength that follows weakness,
as truth instead of lies,
as songtime and springtime
and summertime to be,
    so is my Lord,
    my living Lord,
so is my Lord to me.

2   Like calm in place of clamour,
like peace that follows pain,
like meeting after parting,
like sunshine after rain,
like moonlight and starlight
and sunlight on the sea,
    so is my Lord,
    my living Lord,
so is my Lord to me.

3   As sleep that follows fever,
as gold instead of grey,
as freedom after bondage,
as sunrise to the day,
as home to the traveller
and all we long to see,
    so is my Lord,
    my living Lord,
so is my Lord to me.

29 Light of the minds that know him

WARBURTON 76 76 D

Peter Cutts *b*.1937

1. Light of the minds that know him, may Christ be light to mine! my
sun in ris - en splen - dour, my light of truth di - vine; my
guide in doubt and dark - ness, my true and liv - ing way, my
clear light ev - er shin - ing, my dawn of heav - en's day.

L IGHT of the minds that know him,
may Christ be light to mine!
my sun in risen splendour,
  my light of truth divine;
my guide in doubt and darkness,
  my true and living way,
my clear light ever shining,
  my dawn of heaven's day.

2   Life of the souls that love him,
    may Christ be ours indeed!
  the living bread from heaven
    on whom our spirits feed;
  who died for love of sinners
    to bear our guilty load,
  and make of life's brief journey
    a new Emmaus road.

3   Strength of the wills that serve him,
    may Christ be strength to me,
  who stilled the storm and tempest,
    who calmed the tossing sea;
  his Spirit's power to move me,
    his will to master mine,
  his cross to carry daily
    and conquer in his sign.

4   May it be ours to know him
    that we may truly love,
  and loving, fully serve him
    as serve the saints above;
  till in that home of glory
    with fadeless splendour bright,
  we serve in perfect freedom
    our strength, our life, our light.

based on a prayer of St Augustine

Alternative tunes: AU FORT DE MA DETRESSE
LLANGLOFFAN (*CP* 501)

30 From the night of ages waking

LINGWOOD 87 87 87

C Armstrong Gibbs 1889-1960

1. From the night of a - ges wak-ing morn-ing comes to heart and mind,

day of grace in splen-dour break- ing, mists and sha - dows fall be - hind;

in the bright-ness of his glo-ry Christ the Light of life has shined.

FROM the night of ages waking
  morning comes to heart and mind,
day of grace in splendour breaking,
mists and shadows fall behind;
    in the brightness of his glory
Christ the Light of life has shined.

2 Christ in light immortal dwelling,
   Word by whom the worlds were made;
   Light of lights, our dark dispelling,
   Lord of lords in light arrayed;
       in the brightness of his glory
   see the Father's love displayed.

3 Risen Lord in radiance splendid,
   Christ has conquered Satan's sway;
   sin and shame and sorrow ended,
   powers of darkness flee away;
       in the brightness of his glory
   walk as children of the day.

4 Light to lighten every nation,
   shining forth from shore to shore,
   Christ who won the world's salvation
   now let all the earth adore;
       in the brightness of his glory
   Light of life for evermore.

Alternative tune: REGENT SQUARE (*CP* 502)

INDEX OF TUNES